This book belongs to:

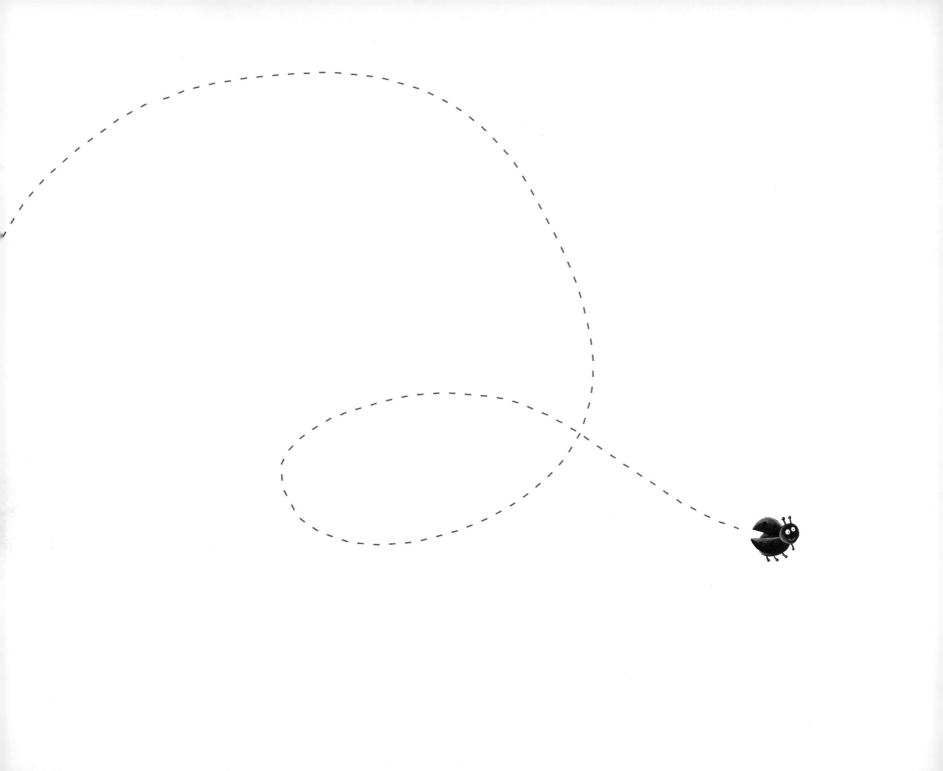

Big Thoughts
for Little People

ABC's to help you grow

Kenneth N. Taylor

ILLUSTRATED BY

Andrea Petrlik Huseinović

Tyndale House Publishers, Inc.
Carol Stream, Illinois

Visit Tyndale's website for kids at www.tyndale.com/kids.

TYNDALE is a registered trademark of Tyndale House Publishers, Inc.

The Tyndale Kids logo is a trademark of Tyndale House Publishers, Inc.

Big Thoughts for Little People: ABC's to Help You Grow

Copyright © 1983 by Kenneth N. Taylor. All rights reserved.

Cover and interior art copyright © 2009 by Andrea Petrlik Huseinović. All rights reserved.

Previously published under ISBN 978-0-842-0164-X.

First repackage edition published in 2009.

Designed by Stephen Vosloo

Scripture quotations are taken from *The Living Bible*, copyright © 1971 by Tyndale House Foundation. Used by permission of Tyndale House Publishers, Inc., Carol Stream, Illinois 60188. All rights reserved.

For manufacturing information regarding this product, please call 1-800-323-9400.

Library of Congress Cataloging-in-Publication Data

Taylor, Kenneth Nathaniel.
  Big thoughts for little people : abc's to help you grow / Kenneth N. Taylor. — 1st repackage ed.
     p. cm.
  Originally published: 1983. With new cover and interior art.
  ISBN 978-1-4143-3310-6 (hc)
  1. Children—Conduct of life. 2. Children—Religious life. I. Title.
  BJ1631.T39 2009
  248.8'2—dc22   2008054254

Printed in China

25   24   23   22   21
10   9   8   7   6

A word to parents (and grandparents)

The following note from Kenneth N. Taylor was included in the first edition of this book. He is now in heaven, but the Big Thoughts he shares from Scripture are still relevant to today's kids.

Many years ago my little book *The Bible in Pictures for Little Eyes* was quietly introduced to Christian parents in America, and now there are a million copies in print in thirty languages around the world. My purpose was to help little children learn about the Bible and God.

This book, *Big Thoughts for Little People*, has a different purpose. Its value is in teaching small children about Christian living—that is, how to be good! This is one of the great themes of the Bible, and it is very important for little children to be taught right from wrong (as well as simple courtesy and good manners).

A word about the wonderful artwork is in order. There are surprises in every picture. For instance, how many ladybugs can you and your child find on the cover? (I see four of them!) There are ladybugs hiding in each illustration. You'll also have fun finding all the objects on each page which begin with the theme letter.

The questions are a very important part of each lesson. Questions that are thought provoking but not hard to answer are of great importance in the learning process.

And please don't skip the Bible verses. Children will learn them easily, and they will stay in the mind and heart for life.

Kenneth N. Taylor

A is for asking.
We ask when we pray.
God is happy to answer
And help us each day.

The children and their father are praying. Can you see them? It is bedtime, and they are talking to God. They are asking God to take care of them, and they are saying, "Thank you" for all the kind things God does for them. God wants us to talk with him. He wants to be our friend. We can pray anytime, wherever we are, because God always hears us.

1. What are the boy and girl and their father doing?

2. If the bears could talk, what would they be thankful for?

3. What are some things you are thankful for? Let's pray now and tell God, "Thank you."

Tell God your needs and don't forget to thank him for his answers.
PHILIPPIANS 4:6

b

B is for **behave**.
It means doing what is right.
Be happy and helpful.
Do not argue or fight.

Do you know what "behave" means? It means doing what your parents ask you to do. It also means playing nicely with other children. In this picture some of the children and animals are behaving and some are not. Look at the girls fighting over an ice cream cone. I think the ice cream cone is going to fall to the ground. Then neither of the girls will have it. But the puppies know better. They are sharing.

1. Are the little girls behaving? What are they doing?

2. Point to the puppies. Are they behaving?

3. What are the children at the table doing?

[Jesus said,] "If you love me, obey me."
JOHN 14:15

C

C is for **crying**.
It hurts when you fall,
But please do not cry
About nothing at all.

Can you see what happened to the boy and girl
on the bicycles? They bumped into each other, and
the girl has fallen off. Ouch! That hurts. Perhaps
she bumped her head. I think she's crying. What
would you do if you fell off? Would you cry? It's all
right to cry if you're hurt. Crying will help you feel
better. But if you're not really hurt, try to smile.
Smiling will also help you feel better.

1. Why is the girl crying?

2. Is it all right to cry if you're hurt?

3. Should you cry every time you get a little bump?

A cheerful heart does good like medicine.
PROVERBS 17:22

D is for doing
What needs to be done.
So please do it cheerfully.
Then you'll have fun.

All these children are doing nice things to help each other. One boy is helping the teacher wash the dishes. He must be careful not to drop and break them. One of the girls is helping by watering the flowers. One of the boys is pulling a girl and her stuffed doggie and bunny in the wagon. We should treat others just as we want them to treat us. God is happy when we do helpful and kind things for one another.

1. What is the duck doing?
2. What are some good things the children are doing? Tell about each one.
3. What kind thing could you do to help someone?

Do for others what you want them to do for you.
MATTHEW 7:12

e

E is for **everyone**.
God loves us all,
The black and the white,
And the short and the tall.

Everyone in the world is special to God. We are all different, but he loves all of us. There are many colors of hair and many colors of skin. Some children are tall, some are short. Some weigh a lot, and some weigh just a little. In some countries, children live in houses or apartments made of wood or stone. In other countries, the children live in houses made of straw or bamboo. Do you see all of the different children playing together in the picture? God loves each one of them.

1. What color is your hair?
2. Find the boy driving the electric train. What color is his hair?
3. Does God love all the children? Does God love you?

See how very much our heavenly Father loves us, for he allows us to be called his children.

1 JOHN 3:1

f

F is for forgiving
A girl or a boy
Who is naughty or careless
And breaks your new toy.

Do you see what the bears have done? They have broken the toy frog. If someone did that to you, you might be angry. Perhaps you would want to get even with him by doing something bad to him. But that isn't the way God wants you to act. He wants you to forgive. He does not want you to hurt people who do something wrong to you. He wants you to be good to them. That is not easy, but God will help you.

1. Look at the children playing in the pool. Which children are fighting?

2. Should those children continue fighting, or should they forgive each other?

3. Did someone hurt you or hurt your feelings today? Did you forgive that person?

Be kind to each other, tenderhearted, forgiving one another.
EPHESIANS 4:32

g

G is for God,
He's your Father above.
He made you and likes you
And shows you his love.

God lives in heaven, far up above the sky, but he is also here with us. Can you see God in the picture? No, we can't see him, but he can see us. He loves us and always wants to help us. He made the earth and sky and flowers and all the animals and people. But even though he is so great and strong, he thinks about us all the time. He wants us to think about him and love him too.

1. Who made the flowers? Who made you?

2. Where is God? Can you see him? Can he see you?

3. Does God love you? Do you love him?

God looked over all that he had made, and it was excellent in every way.
GENESIS 1:31

H is for helping
Your mom or your dad.
It says in the Bible
That this makes God glad.

God tells us in the Bible to be kind to others and to help them. Sometimes that isn't easy, because we want to do things to please ourselves instead of helping others. Look at all the children in the picture who are helping. Some are helping collect eggs. Others are helping with the animals. God wants us to be cheerful helpers. That means not to complain when you are asked to help. God will teach you how to be a cheerful helper if you ask him to.

1. Point to all the children who are helping. What is each one doing?

2. Were you a helper today? What did you do?

3. What can you do tomorrow to be a helper? Ask your mom or dad to remind you to be a helper.

God will bless you and use you to help others.
1 TIMOTHY 4:16

I is for illness,
Which may keep you in bed.
But soon you feel fine
And are playing instead.

It is no fun to be sick, but it happens to all of us once in a while. Usually you feel better soon, but sometimes you need to go to the doctor to get medicine or a shot. You might even have to go to the hospital. Some children live where there aren't very many doctors to help. In those places the children are sick more often and sometimes it takes much longer for them to get well. We should thank God for doctors and pray for people in places where there are not very many doctors.

1. Have you ever been sick?

2. Did you go to the doctor?

3. What did the doctor do?

I was . . . sick . . . and you visited me.
MATTHEW 25:36

j

J is for joyful,
It means full of cheer.
Have fun and be happy
Each day of the year.

Christmas is a joyful time. It is the celebration of Jesus' birthday. It reminds us about God and how much he loves us. We decorate Christmas trees and give presents to each other. We like to sing Christmas carols. We can also be joyful every day of the year. We can thank God for our families. We can play with our friends. We can help other people. These things all make us joyful.

1. What kind of tree is in the picture?

2. Are the children in the picture being joyful or sad?

3. What are some things that make you joyful?

Always be full of joy in the Lord.
PHILIPPIANS 4:4

k

K is for **k**indness
To Grandpa and Gram.
Be helpful to others.
Be sweet as a lamb!

These children are visiting their grandparents and are being kind to them and the neighborhood kids. Being kind means being friendly to people and helping them. Some people are mean and not kind at all. They want everything for themselves. They don't stop to think about what other people want. When they act that way, they are being unkind. But God wants us to help others and to be friendly to them. He wants us to be kind.

1. How do you feel when you have been mean and unkind?

2. Tell about something you did to be kind to someone.

3. Does God want you to be kind or unkind?

You should practice tenderhearted mercy and kindness to others.
COLOSSIANS 3:12

L is for lying,
A thing not to do.
No matter what happens,
Only say what is true.

Look at the broken window. The boy's baseball went through the window. Have you ever broken something and then said you didn't do it? That would be lying instead of telling the truth, and God does not like lies. I hope the boy tells the truth about the broken window. Why do people tell lies? I think it is because they don't want to be scolded or punished for what they have done. But God wants us to tell the truth, even if it means we will be punished.

1. What happened to the window?

2. Does God want us to tell lies?

3. Can you think of a time when you wanted to tell a lie, but you told the truth instead?

You must not lie.
EXODUS 20:16

m

M is for **messy**,
With toys on the floor.
So put them away,
In a box or a drawer.

Some boys and girls leave their toys on the floor where people can fall over them and get hurt and break the toys. Wouldn't it be better to pick up the toys and put them away when you are through playing with them? Usually this makes everyone happier. It is also good to make your bed look neat in the morning and after a nap. And you can clear the table after meals and help wash and dry the dishes so they won't be messy.

1. What is the girl doing to her bed?
2. What should the children do with the toys on the floor?
3. Do you pick up your toys when you are finished playing with them?

God is not one who likes things to be disorderly and upset.
1 CORINTHIANS 14:33

N is for **n**ice.
Being nice is worthwhile.
Be pleasant to others
And give them a smile.

Do your parents ever tell you to be nice? What do they mean? Perhaps you have been playing too roughly, or you hit someone, or you've been quarreling. When they tell you to be nice they mean you should stop doing those things. They want you to be pleasant and helpful. When you are nice, everyone is happy. When you do something naughty, everyone is sad.

1. Did you do anything today that wasn't nice? What was it?

2. Did you do something nice today? What was it?

3. What can you do tomorrow to be nice?

Happy are the kind and merciful.
MATTHEW 5:7

Miss

Nancy

1 2 3 4 5 6 7 8 9

n N

O

O is for **o**bey.
When you do as you're told,
It makes parents glad.
They won't punish or scold.

God tells us to obey our parents. He says this is very important because our parents know what is best for us. We will be happiest if we obey our parents. God says that fathers and mothers should discipline their children when they don't obey. If you are punished, it will help you remember to obey your parents. And after they have punished you, your parents will give you a big hug and will tell you how much they love you. Then everyone will be happy.

1. What kind of fruit is growing on the trees?

2. What does God say your parents should do if you don't obey?

3. Who is happy when you obey?

Children, obey your parents; this is the right thing to do.
EPHESIANS 6:1

p

P is for **polite**,
Saying, "Thank you,"
and, "Please."
It is not hard to do
And puts others at ease.

When someone is at ease, that person feels comfortable and happy. Being polite makes other people feel happy. When you ask for something, it is more polite to say, "May I please have it?" than to say, "Gimme that!" And when someone gives you something, it is polite to say, "Thank you." Being polite shows respect. That means you think the other person is as good as you are, or even better. God wants us to respect other people, so he likes it when we are polite. He doesn't want us to think we are better than others.

1. Point to the children in the picture who are being polite.

2. Tell about some ways you can be polite.

3. Does God want us to be polite? Why?

Kind words are like honey—enjoyable and healthful.
PROVERBS 16:24

q

Q is for **quarrel**.
Each wants the first turn.
But waiting for others
Is not hard to learn.

Oh, dear me! Look at the children who are quarreling. Each one is mad at someone else! Is this good? No! These children are being selfish and want things for themselves instead of taking turns. Is there a way to solve their problem? I hope someone shows them how to play nicely together, like some of the other children are doing. You can learn to be kind to your playmates. Then they will learn to be kind too. You can be the one to show them how.

1. Why are some of the children in the picture quarreling?

2. Do you ever quarrel? About what?

3. How can you stop a quarrel?

Quarreling, harsh words, and dislike of others should have no place in your lives.
EPHESIANS 4:31

R is for **resting**,
Like taking a nap,
Or sometimes just sitting
On Mother's soft lap.

Sometimes we all need to stop working or playing to take a rest. That is the way God made us. He wants us to be rested because then we are happier. If you don't get enough rest you will probably be upset and unhappy. Then everyone else will be unhappy too. Nap time is a good time. You can lie in bed and think pleasant thoughts, and all of a sudden you'll be asleep. Then when you wake up you'll be happy as a songbird. Maybe you will sing!

1. How many children in the picture are resting?

2. Why do you feel better after your nap?

3. What can happen when you get too tired?

God wants his loved ones to get their proper rest.
PSALM 127:2

S

S is for **s**inging.
We sing when we're glad.
It might even help
If you sing when you're sad.

Everyone likes to sing. There are happy songs and sad songs, funny songs and serious songs. We can sing while we play or while we take a walk. Some people like to sing in the bathtub or in the shower. God likes to hear us sing. He made us with voices that can sing. Singing makes us happy, and God wants us to be happy. Singing can even help us feel happy when we are sad. I hope you know lots of songs.

1. Which child is dressed up like a ladybug?

2. Do you like to sing?

3. What are some songs you know?

[Sing] to the Lord with thankful hearts.
COLOSSIANS 3:16

T is for thankful.
Thank God for your lunch.
And thank him for dinner
And breakfast and brunch.

The children in the picture are thanking God for their food. Many children in the world don't have enough to eat. They are hungry all the time. But others have good breakfasts and lunches and suppers, and sometimes even snacks in between. We should thank God every day for the food we are able to eat. God is pleased when we bow our heads before we eat and say, "Thank you" to him.

1. What are some things you are thankful for?

2. Who are some people you are thankful for?

3. When should we thank God for food?

Thank the Lord for all the glorious things he does.
PSALM 105:1

God bless our friends everywhere

U is for **u**nselfish.
Be willing to share.
Be thoughtful of others
And always be fair.

A selfish person wants the first turn, the biggest cookie, and the best of everything. But an unselfish person is willing to let others go first or have the biggest cookie. When you share with your friends, you have more fun together. Sometimes it is very difficult, but God wants us to be unselfish, so that is the best thing to do. It is better to please God than to please ourselves. One good thing about sharing is that an unselfish person is happier than a selfish person.

1. Who is riding a unicycle?

2. Does God want us to be selfish or unselfish?

3. Can you think of some ways you can be unselfish?

Don't think only of yourself. Try to think of the other fellow, too, and what is best for him.
1 CORINTHIANS 10:24

V

V is for **v**isitors.
Help them have fun,
And play and be friendly
With all, not just one.

It is wonderful to have friends. You can go to their houses to visit, or they can come to visit you. Sometimes you can eat lunch together, or you can play outside or have fun making things. When you have visitors you must remember to play happily together and take turns with your toys. And remember to play with each of your visitors, not just the ones you like best. Then everyone will have fun.

1. How many children in the picture are coming to visit?

2. Tell the names of your friends who come to your house to visit.

3. What are some things you do together?

Cheerfully share your home with those who need a meal or a place to stay for the night.
1 PETER 4:9

W

W is for **worship.**
That means giving God praise
And telling our love for him
All of our days.

When you think about how great and good God is, and how much you love him, then you are worshiping him. You can thank God and worship him at church, or at home, or when you are all alone. Yes, you can talk to God wherever you are. You can think about how wonderful he is because he made the trees and grass and stars and sun and moon. And you can tell him, "Thank you" for making you and loving you.

1. In the picture, which things did God make?

2. Who loves you even more than your parents do?

3. Tonight when you go to bed you can worship God by thanking him for loving you and for making the sun and stars.

All the earth shall worship you and sing of your glories.
PSALM 66:4

X

X is for **x**ylophone.
Use it to play
Happy songs about Jesus
Throughout each new day.

Look at all the musical instruments in this picture. Can you find the xylophones? Have you ever played a xylophone? It makes pretty music, but it sounds very different from a piano or a violin. Do you think God likes to hear children play a xylophone? I think he does. God likes music. He especially likes it when we play or sing songs about him. He wants us to tell him how much we love him.

1. Have you ever played a xylophone?

2. What other instruments are the children playing?

3. Does God like to hear children making music?

Make a joyful symphony before the Lord, the King!
PSALM 98:6

y

Y is for **yelling.**
It's all right outdoors,
But please be **more quiet**
In houses and stores.

Do you like to yell? I think most children do.
Sometimes making a lot of noise is all right, but
sometimes it isn't. Here are some times you should
be quiet:
When your mother is resting or is tired.
When the baby is asleep.
When your parents have guests.
When you should be taking a nap.

1. Can you find someone taking a nap in a hammock?

2. Do you see someone in the tree?

3. When should you be quiet?

If you shout a pleasant greeting to a
friend too early in the morning, he will
count it as a curse!
PROVERBS 27:14

Z is for zebra
Or zebu or zoo.
God made all the creatures,
And he made you, too.

Do you know what a zoo is? It is a place where there are many, many kinds of animals and birds and snakes. There are even lions and tigers and bears. Sometimes there are zebus, which are like cows with a hump and floppy ears. Have you ever been to a zoo? If so, you know there are many kinds of animals. See if you can find some of them in the picture. Did you know that God made all these animals? God made the grass and trees and rocks and animals, and he made you a very special person.

1. Where are the zebras in the picture?

2. Which animals can the children pet?

3. Who made all the animals?

[The Lord said,] "By my great power I have made the earth and all mankind and every animal."
JEREMIAH 27:5

About the Author

Kenneth N. Taylor is best known as the translator of *The Living Bible*, but his first renown was as a writer of children's books. Ken and his wife, Margaret, had ten children, and his early books were written for use in the family's daily devotions. The manuscripts were ready for publication only when they passed the scrutiny of those ten young critics! Those books, which have now been read to four generations of children around the world, include *The Bible in Pictures for Little Eyes* (Moody Press), *Stories for the Children's Hour* (Moody Press), and *Taylor's Bible Story Book* (Tyndale House). Now the Taylor children are all grown, so *Big Thoughts for Little People* was written with the numerous grandchildren in mind.

Ken Taylor was a graduate of Wheaton College and Northern Baptist Seminary. He was the founder and chairman of Tyndale House Publishers, Inc. He died in 2005 at the age of eighty-eight.

About the Illustrator

Andrea Petrlik Huseinović was born in Zagreb, Croatia, and attended the School of Applied Arts and the Academy of Fine Arts. She is an award-winning illustrator of over forty books for Croatian and international publishers, and is the author of four picture books, *The Blue Sky, My Family, Ciconia Ciconia (White Stork),* and *Maleni,* which have been translated into several languages. Andrea remembers the original *Big Thoughts for Little People* from her childhood. She lives in Croatia.